CELEBRATING OURSELVES

"...and the old women keep the beat!"

Celebrating Ourselves:
A Crone Ritual Book

EDITED BY EDNA M. WARD
Illustrated by Sylvia Sims

Portland   Maine

Astarte Shell Press
P. O. Box 10453
Portland, Maine 04104

Copyright 1992 by Edna M. Ward
All rights reserved

No part of this book may be used or reproduced in any manner whatsoever without written permission except in the case of brief quotations embodied in critical articles and reviews.

Grateful acknowledgement is made to the following for permission to reprint previously published materials:

HarperCollins Publishers, Inc. for reprinting "the circle is open" chant from TRUTH OR DARE: ENCOUNTERS WITH POWER, AUTHORITY, AND MYSTERY by Starhawk (San Francisco: Harper & Row, 1987). Copyright 1987 by Miriam Simos.

Susan Savell for reprinting "and the old women keep the beat" from "Keep Simple Ceremonies" by Susan Savell, ASCAP. Copyright by Ritual Music Publishing Co.

Library of Congress Cataloging-in-Publication Data
Celebrating Ourselves: A Crone ritual book
Edna M. Ward, editor; Sylvia Sims, illustrator.
   p.   cm.
Includes bibliographical references.
ISBN 0-9624626-3-2 (pbk.): $6.00
1. Ritual 2. Aged woman—religious life I. Ward, Edna M.,   1928—
BL625. 7.C45   1992
291.3' 8' 0846—dc20   92-22760
                                            CIP

Printed in the U.S. by Coastal Business Center, Wiscasset, Maine

1st Printing 1992

10 9 8 7 6 5 4 3 2 1

TABLE OF CONTENTS

INTRODUCTION 1

THE CRONE RITUAL AND COMMUNITY 3

THE RITUAL 13

CRONES PAST AND PRESENT 25

THE CRONES

Lou Bennett
Helen Brigham
Martha Dares
Joanna Faust
Irene Fidryeht
Mickey Furnas
Alice Gifford
Elly Haney
Alysan Hooper
Nancy Hutchison
Bobbie Keppel
Lorraine Latour

Debbie Leighton
Nancy Nutt
Holly Odell
Jean Parker
Betty Peterson
Alice Pratt
Charlotte Ritter
Sylvia Sims
Anita Talbot
Edna Ward
Enid Tiger Williams
Betty Wurtz

INTRODUCTION

The crone ritual has been a celebration of the Feminist Spiritual Community (FSC) of Portland, Maine, since 1982. Twenty-four women have celebrated the passage to old age through this ritual. Word has gotten out that there is a ceremony that values and honors old women!

Aging is like the maturing of a fine wine.
--Debbie

The crone members of the Community are entrusted with the ritual. We all share leadership for its celebration, and change it as new insights come to us. In response to the interest in and longing for something positive to mark the journey into old age, we have now decided to put the ritual into writing and to share with a wider circle something of its meaning for us. We are aware that in writing it down, the ritual will become something different. It will no longer be embedded in the vibrant life of a community in which it has meaning, value and power. But we trust that as it evolves in the lives of other communities, it will enrich and sustain women in new and exciting ways.

We invited all those who have become crones through this ritual to contribute to the book. Many responded, sharing their stories and memories, as well as writing and revising sections. This book is a result of that collaborative process.

The ritual itself is the center of the book. Everything else supports it. The first chapter sets the context—the community in which it is celebrated—and our reflection on its significance. The second chapter describes the ritual itself, the participants and the ritual objects of importance to us. The following chapter provides some further resources for reflection and discussion about our heritage, about aging and ageism and about possibilities for the future. A bibliography is included at the end. In sharing this ritual with you, we are very much aware that it has emerged out of the life of a particular community, one whose members are currently almost all of Euro-American working and middle-class backgrounds and who live in Maine. We have drawn on heritages, memories and experiences important to us. The order and components of the ritual and the objects we use have meaning, value and power to us.

Your contexts and herstories may be quite different from ours. The role of old women and even the understanding of when one becomes old in your communities will shape your rituals in specific, rich and unique ways.

We share this ritual with you, therefore, not at all as a model but as a resource or simply an example of the wealth of possibilities for alternative ceremonies. It has blessed us, and we share it in that spirit. If it fits with your interests and needs, if it can be of use, it is yours to do with as you wish.

Some of you may feel that you do not have a community with which to celebrate such a ritual. We encourage you to think of your friends or family, a church or temple, an activist or study group and consider adapting this one or creating a different one for that context.

In love and solidarity with old women everywhere, we offer this ritual.

THE CRONE RITUAL AND COMMUNITY

The Crone Ritual in the Feminist Spiritual Community

The crone ritual in this book was developed by the Feminist Spiritual Community of Portland, Maine. The Community, as we call it, was started in 1980 by a group of about fifteen women who wished to create and celebrate rituals, support one another in our personal and political struggles and study and act together.

We gather on Monday evenings for at least two hours at the Friends Meeting House in Portland. We sit in a circle around a center, or altar. We sit on the floor or on cushions or in low beach chairs. The altar is a simple cloth with designs of significance to the Community. Candles, shells and stones, flowers or a plant, crystals and other objects are placed on the cloth. On any given evening, special objects are added—a postcard from a member working on a tanker, a candle for a member in jail.

Between twenty and thirty women usually attend. On Mondays, the focus is ritual and support. In addition, we offer workshops and courses, we initiate actions on specific justice issues, and we have become a sister to a repatriated village in El Salvador. Once a month, on "Third Moonday," we meet before ritual for business.

Each Monday's ritual is organized around a theme; the leadership for it is widely shared. Women sign up on a ritual calendar months in advance to explore, commemorate or celebrate a special event or theme. We have had rituals of sending for members going to Central America and Big Mountain. We have explored countless themes, including goddess traditions, women's lives, friendships, power, justice, the future and work. We have regularly celebrated the passage of the seasons and the Community's birthday. We have rituals blessing babies, celebrating name changes and partnerships, honoring separations and other personal milestones. And we celebrate the passage into old age, which we call cronehood.

We define cronehood by two characteristics—menopause and age fifty-six. A crone is a woman who has reached her fifty-sixth birthday and who has entered menopause. In selecting age fifty-six, we follow Z. Budapest's astrological calculation that by that age, Saturn, the teaching planet, has returned twice to a woman.[1]

We first celebrated this passage in 1982. We decided to honor the two women of the Community who had become crones – one of Franco-American, working-class background who had retired from the postal service and had begun working on a college degree, and a middle-class, Anglo-American woman, who was a pre-school teacher and peace activist.

One of our members, artist Gina Kelley, designed the ritual. She also built a cardboard gate framed by a tree and a female figure, through which we passed and formed a circle. The ritual continued with a series of questions and answers, read by different members, about the meaning and history of cronehood; a meditation; an exercise we call the "decades;" and an acknowledgment of the passage into cronehood.[2] In turn, the two crones spoke of what that passage meant to them.

Over the years, the ritual has been changed slightly, and it is still evolving. We have omitted the question and answer format and replaced it with a simple presentation. We have added a section on gifts and one of preparation for the ceremony.

Twenty-four women have become crones. Fifteen are Community members. The others live elsewhere, in Maine, Massachusetts, Rhode Island and Pennsylvania. Twenty-three are white, of diverse ethnic backgrounds. One is African-American. We are divided between traditional middle and working-class backgrounds. In age, we range from the late fifties to the late seventies. We are eclectic spiritually and theologically, including church members, witches and nature mystics among us (those categories are not mutually exclusive ones!). We are peace and justice activists; artists, teachers, therapists, social workers, carpenters, printers, homemakers; mothers, daughters, lovers, friends. We identify ourselves as bi-sexual, lesbian or straight, and some of us find those categories pretty confusing.

Most of us have had diverse lives: as a Catholic sister who left the order, married and now runs a small printing business; as homemaker and mother who embarked on a college education after her children were grown; as a college professor; as an advertising executive. Several of us broke ground in traditional male fields—as the first women vice president of her college, the first woman professor in religion at another college, the first woman custodian for a local high school.

Many of us were active in the movements for racial justice in the fifties and sixties and have continued in that struggle, adding the other movements—feminism, peace, justice for the earth—as they evolved. We continue to take on the challenges of contemporary injustices as we have come to see the connections among them all. And although our social analysis varies, we seem to become increasingly radical as we have grown older.

The Significance of the Crone Ritual

A crone ritual evening is one of high, joyful energy and visual beauty. Preparation for the ceremony and the ritual itself are elaborate and detailed. It attracts a large group, and it has become one of the most significant rituals of the Community. Its importance suggests to us that it has responded to a profound spiritual/personal/political emptiness in this society.

In the dominant culture, there are three major ritual occasions available to old people—retirement from a job or career, birthdays and marriage anniversaries. None contains an intrinsically positive interpretation of aging. Indeed, birthdays often reinforce the normative value of youth, a value reflected in the birthday cards in any card shop. Marriage anniversaries are generally positive and celebrative, but they are limited to those who are married and are not really about aging. Retirement occasions may also honor and even celebrate the person retiring, but they are essentially negative about age and are limited to those in certain areas of the paid workforce. The negativity of such occasions is sufficiently seen in its name—retirement. It is an occasion to leave something, to honor the contributions that have been made. It is focused on what a person is going from, not to. It is not a passage so much as an ending.

Such assumptions, beliefs, values, policies and practices, reflected in and justified by such occasions, help to make up what is called ageism.³ Ageism is a structure of institutional and personal power, beliefs, values, policies and practices that places high value on young adulthood and renders both the old and the very young expendable and marginal. It makes us into not fully human objects that may be cute, unpleasant and burdensome, ignored or—for a few minutes—enjoyed. It leaves many of us with little income and less security and power. It subjects us to emotional and physical neglect, abuse and violence.

Nationally, several organizations have arisen to challenge aspects of ageism. The Grey Panthers, Older Women's League (OWL), Senior Corps of Retired Executives (SCORE), American Association of Retired Persons (AARP) and the Displaced Homemakers Program are a few that lobby for the interests of the old, offer means of gaining a liveable income and provide an avenue for continuing service to the wider community.

The social analyses, politics and constituencies of those organizations are, of course, diverse. In addition, none includes a spiritual dimension as an intrinsic part of its identity. And the immediate popularity of our crone ritual suggests that such a dimension is terribly important, that we need rituals of aging that celebrate this stage of a life journey in a religious context, that support and prepare one for the next stages—including death— and that contribute also to challenging the prevailing ageism of the culture.

For those of us who are crones, who have been honored by the Community's ritual, this ritual helps to provide this essential missing piece. It is a spiritual ritual; i.e., it is a source and mediator of value, meaning and power. It affirms us. It celebrates us. It authenticates our lives as old women and/or as women getting older. We are given crystals and stoles as symbols of our new status. A crone candle is kept by the Community and brought out and placed in the center of the altar each time a crone ritual is celebrated. Friends and family are invited on this special night, and they, along with members of the Community, give us gifts—both material items and wishes. We are honored for being who we are—women fifty-six years and older.

In valuing us, the ritual offers us new meaning and identities. It also redefines old age itself. The ritual is a rite of passage, a gate into still another phase of our journeys. It reflects this redefinition in several ways. The gate, designed for our first ritual, is a major symbol. Two others are the birthing canal and the decades. We make a birthing canal with our bodies and pass through it, coming into a new life. We are giving birth to something new. Similarly, in the activity known as the decades, we take turns sharing important images and stories of our lives from each decade we have lived. Always the stories change with the decades, and as each decade is superseded by a later one, the momentum builds. We continue to move into the future, onward and onward. The sixties become a time, not of retiring or fading away but another decade of full, dramatic, valuable life. As the seventies can become...and the eighties...and the nineties....

> *I am beginning to realize the wealth of wisdom I have, from living, not from scholarship.*
> —Edna

The ritual has spiritual significance also by connecting this occasion and this individual life with a larger matrix of value and meaning. The ritual affirms that "*this is the way it should be,*" or in conventional religious terms, "*this has the blessing of god or goddesses.*" The language that is used throughout, the values it embodies and the joy and excitement that attend it all communicate a transcendent blessing.

In and through all the above, the ritual mediates power as well as value and meaning. Many of us experience a new freedom to be and do and a new capacity to act. It not only affirms and symbolizes what we are becoming. It helps us to become and to be.

The ritual both reflects and helps to establish a matrix of support for our ongoing journeys. We can share our stories and experiences, our pain and crises, our joys and discoveries with our sister crones. We are not alone; we journey together even as we journey separately. It is such a comfort and thrill to be able to go to Community on any Monday night and see others who also name themselves crone!

Further, every time we celebrate the crone ritual and celebrate a new crone, we challenge an ageist culture with its oppression and violence. We challenge the way it has been internalized in each one of us. Each celebration is a basic step in and declaration of shedding ourselves of internalized ageism.

The power mediated by the ritual has a social as well as individual dimension. It challenges the ageism of the other Community women and the family and friends who attend for the evening. In preparing for the ritual, we explore in small groups how ageism shapes our lives and our roles in perpetuating it. The ritual then celebrates an alternative way of understanding old age.

And it helps to legitimate that alternative. As the

> *At age 60, I just now feel that I have really come into my own. I feel very privileged to have lived this long.*
> —Elly

ritual is re-enacted, as the passage is indeed ritualized, it becomes authoritative. It becomes a warrant for viewing old age differently from the way the dominant culture does and for acting differently. Ritual carries authority; it invests an action, a story, an event, a hope—whatever is ritualized—with meaning, legitimacy and value.

Finally, the stories of our experiences of ageism and/or of challenging it and our stories of our continuing journeys become part of the lore of the Community. They become part of the subversive knowledge that remains a catalyst for change — for changing ourselves and the wider society.

The Significance of the Crone Ritual in Community

Our experience is not only that a crone ritual is of paramount importance today. It is also that the ritual must be grounded in community. Much of what has already been written assumes that the ritual is embedded in the warp and woof of community.

Community deepens and sustains the meaning, value and power of the ritual. We can come to this Community on any Monday evening and be with other crones. We have become a circle of our own within the larger circle, and it is our special responsibility to prepare and lead the Crone ritual for new women.

Further, we are constantly surrounded by a "cloud of witnesses" to our cronehood—our sister crones and also all the other women in the Community who have participated in, or even heard about, the ritual. We are surrounded by the legacy of the stories Community women have shared about age and aging in this culture. They are woven into our memories; they help shape the way we relate to one another; they inform our visions, plans and business of the Community.

In the Community we have an opportunity to continue to share of ourselves, our experiences, our insights and wisdom. Actually, it is more than an opportunity; there is an expectation, an unspoken assumption that we will share and that we will provide leadership as much as we want to. We are a part of the Community with all the same rights and responsibilities as anyone else. And although ageism is not absent from the Community, we are genuinely respected and valued for all that and who we are.

A community is necessary if the ritual is to have lasting political power in the wider society. Rituals have to be institutionalized; they can't simply float free, although they may begin that way. The ritual of baptism has lasted because it has a home in the church. The ritual of marriage has lasted for many reasons, but one is that it has a home in both religious and legal institutions. Both rituals are grounded somewhere. They become a part of an institution's identity and responsibility. The become part of an institution's legacy.

Further, a ritual must be community-specific. The ritual described here has power, meaning and value for us as white women who are still relatively young crones. In communities of color, for instance, in which old women have typically played quite different roles from those we are familiar with and who may have been named old at a different age, rituals of passage will be richly distinctive and intrinsic to those communities.

Finally, as such rituals become institutionalized, their authority develops and gradually reaches out to challenge the rituals or lack of rituals in the wider society. As they continue to speak to a very real and felt need, their power to challenge ageism will increase.

THE RITUAL

In the Community, the crone ritual continues to change and evolve. Of the many that we have held, no two have been exactly the same. What follows is simply the most recent version. The objects we use and the outline of the ceremony are listed first and then described in more detail on the following pages.

* Enfolding: welcoming one another

   Birthing Canal: dancing through a gate or arches into a new way of life

* Lighting of Candles: remembering and honoring women near and far

* Naming Circle: casting our circle

   Preparation for Celebration: exploring the treatment of old women by the dominant society

   Who Is a Crone? Why Celebrate Her?: introducing the ritual occasion

* Guided meditation

   Decades: sharing the pain, violence, struggles and joys of each decade of our lives

   Crone Circle: crones share their stories

   Giving of Gifts: giving stoles and crystals and other gifts to new crones

   Dancing: crones leading the Community in drumming, chanting and dancing

CELEBRATING OURSELVES

Feasting: sharing bread and juice

* Singing: making a joyful noise

* Benediction: opening the circle out to the world.

*Starred activities are traditionally used each Monday night.

If you plan to include most or all of these activities, you should allow at least two and one-half hours. If we have more than one or two women to be celebrated, we generally omit the meditation.

Ritual Objects Altar, or center cloth
Candles
Flowers, herbs, plants
Stoles
Crystals
Food
Special objects of significance to the Community or crones.

The Ritual Described

Enfolding

We usually all line up outside the ritual room. As each woman enters the room, she is welcomed by name and with a hug by two greeters at the door. Passing on into the room, the women form a circle around the altar cloth.

Birthing Canal

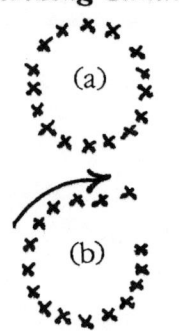

The designated crone begins chanting, *"We are women giving birth to ourselves"* (a). This chant is taken up by everyone in the circle and continues throughout this whole sequence. The crone takes the hand of the woman to her right, breaks the circle and leads the group in a snake dance to another part of the room or around the room until the original circle no longer exists (b). The crone and the next woman then stand opposite each other, forming the beginning of two lines facing

THE RITUAL

each other and reach up to form an arch with their hands held high (c). The line behind the two move through the arch, and each succeeding pair adds to the arch until the whole line has gone through and formed a symbolic birth canal (d).

Now we are ready to give birth to ourselves! We sometimes change the chant here to *"we are women giving birth to our new selves."* Taking her partner's hand, the designated crone leads her through the canal (e). Each of the pairs follows suit until the whole line has gone through. Still holding hands, we once again form a circle and then sit around the crone altar cloth (f).

Traditionally we light three candles, the first for *"all the women attending the meeting for the first time";* the second for *"those who cannot be present tonight";* and the third for *"all of us who are here."* After these, other candles may be lit. At the croning ceremony, we light a large lavender candle for the crones. We sometimes light votive candles encircling the cloth in memory of other crones. Members are asked by the leaders of the evening ritual to light all except the votive candles. For these, participants are simply invited to honor any old women they choose to by lighting a candle.

Lighting Candles

Beginning with the ritual leader, each one, in turn, states her name, brings to the circle other women in spirit and, if she wishes, asks for energy or help or offers her energy and help to others. Participants are often invited to bring other crones to the circle. As each woman names herself, she takes the hand of the woman to her left, and so on around the circle. At the end, the ritual leader usually suggests a few moments of silence to allow the energy to flow through all of us and especially to those in need.

Naming Circle

CELEBRATING OURSELVES

Preparation for Celebration Before we honor the new crones, we divide into small circles of three or four to share images and experiences of old age in this society. Usually we are given specific questions: *what are some of the major images of old women in this society? Are there different ones for different groups, e.g., poor white women, middle class white women, poor black women? What stories do you wish to share about the lives of old women today?* We then bring these to the large circle and briefly share them with a summary of major themes and images.

We include this component because it is important to remember the pain and violence of old age as well as its joys, to remind ourselves that old age is a social/political reality and not simply a natural one, and to gain insights into our feelings and actions about old people.

Who is a Crone? Why Celebrate Her? A crone explains to the group what a crone is and why we celebrate the attainment of this stage of a woman's life. She may summarize some of the themes identified in the Preparation component above, as well as mention cultures in which old women are honored and play significant roles in the community.

She suggests some of the ways feminists can rename and revalue old women. Three areas in particular of women's lives are often identified:

 a) Bodily changes—we are learning to see menopause not only as an ending but also a beginning.

 b) Changing relationships—we are learning to see ourselves and others, the changes in our relationships, plans for the future and our own mortality from new perspectives.

c) Years of experience—we are learning to respect pain and struggles and to search for the wisdom in them.

We honor these passages. We celebrate the rich gifts of a woman's life and support her in risk-taking as she moves forward into life and death and life.

A crone leads the Community in a meditation. One that we sometimes use is included on p. 20.

Guided Meditation

Following the preceding presentation, we stand in a circle to begin a very special part of the crone ritual called *"the Decades."* Through the process of the Decades, we see a shape of each woman's story emerge with its sorrows, pain, joy, aspirations and achievements.

The Decades

Starting with the decade from age ten to nineteen, we go around the circle saying a few words, phrases or sentences that capture the flavor of that decade as we have experienced it. Participants should be urged to be brief! The idea is to name something significant about the decade. What is said may be positive or negative and anyone can pass if she desires. For some, a painfully simple statement like *"I survived"* will suffice.

After everyone has given her response to the decade of the teens, those who have left that decade take a step forward toward the center, leaving behind those who are not yet twenty. Again, each in turn voices an image, phrase, sentence that characterizes that decade.

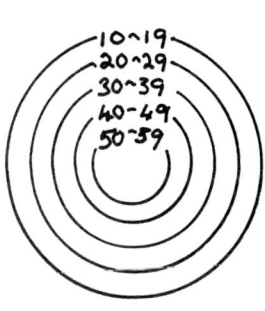

This continues for each decade until the decade of the fifties is finished. Then the crones and initiate crones step into the innermost circle.

The Decades generates a lot of emotion. It is not unusual to find that the decades of the thirties and forties, in particular, are filled with turmoil and then improve with the fifties.

Crone Circle Having reached the inner circle, the crones sit in a circle while everyone else forms a circle around them. The old crones shower the new ones with such affirmations as:

> *You are honored and beloved women!*
> *You have lived long and survived!*
> *You have made a difference in the world!*
> *You have a wealth of stories and ideas to share!*

The old crones then speak briefly about what it is like being a crone. And the new crones are asked such questions as:

> *How does it feel to be honored as a crone?*
> *What stories would you like to share tonight?*
> *What fears, hopes, dreams, plans do you have*
> *   for the future?*
> *What do you need from us?*

If there are only one or two new crones, you may wish to show slides/pictures of their lives or invite others to share stories, memories, images of the new crones. How you choose to honor them is limited only by your imagination.

Giving of Gifts After each new crone has responded, the old crones give them two gifts. The first is a stole, which is worn at crone ceremonies. It is presented with such words as *"as a symbol of your new status, we present you with this stole, weaving together the strands of your life."* The second gift is an amethyst

THE RITUAL

crystal, with the words, *"the Community supports you in your journey forward. We praise and bless you, we look to learn from you. We give you amethyst crystals to help you in your ongoing transformation."*

We also then present another crystal, a special meditation crystal, to one of the new crones, to be passed around among them until the next crone ceremony.

The ritual leader turns to the wider circle and asks if there are other gifts of words and objects to be presented. Many usually express appreciation and thanks for the new crones, and some bring special objects to them.

After all gifts have been given, one of the old crones shouts, *"The old women keep the beat,"* and she starts beating a drum. The crones join hands and begin the chant, which is taken up by the whole group. *"The old women keep the beat! The old women keep the beat!"* The lead crone moves out of the circle and begins a spiraling dance, the rest of the women following her, chanting and beating drums. When a circle is again formed, everyone joins hands and runs to the center with a loud *"whoop!"* and back out again.

Dancing

As women who bake bread across the world, we break bread together. Platters of homemade sweet bread are passed around the circle, along with juice or water.

Feasting

Singing is one of the most cherished activities of the Community. FSC ends every meeting with singing, hands joined in a weave of women.

Singing

Benediction/ Opening the Circle

We always end with:

*The circle is open but unbroken.
May the peace of the goddess go in your hearts,
Merry meet and merry part,
And merry meet again.*[4]

A Crone Meditation

Sometimes we include a guided meditation if we have only one or two women becoming crones. One of the present crones leads the meditation. She introduces it by asking everyone to get comfortable—usually lying down or sitting. She also reminds us that if images or thoughts should arise during the meditation that are painful or harmful, one should stop participating and just wait until others are through.

We generally begin with a brief relaxing exercise and then proceed into the meditation. This is one that we have done often. (The dots represent pauses.) Don't rush a meditation. Give people time to enter into the experience.

It is warm.... The smell is sweet and pungent....

You come to a large tree with a hole in it. You look in and see a ladder going down. You climb down, unafraid but curious.... At the bottom there is a door with a bright brass knob. You turn the knob and the door opens into a lovely landscape...warm...sunny...with birds, flowers, trees....

You walk along a path that takes you toward

THE RITUAL

water.... Sitting on a rock at the edge of the water is a crone...a wise older woman. She looks very familiar. She is about your size. Her position is one that you frequently take. You approach her, and as she turns to look at you, you realize that you are looking at yourself....

She rises, opens her arms to greet you.

How do you describe this woman? What words do you use?...what colors?.... What music does she make you think of?....

You move toward her...embrace her...together you begin to walk.... You talk. She tells you what is important in her life...what she likes to do...what her burdens are....

You continue on your journey with your friend. You walk to a meadow where there are birds and flowers. She stoops and picks a flower and gives it to you. She directs you to ask the flower what special gift you shall have as a crone....

When it is time for you to make your return journey, you slowly walk back along the path to the tree and ladder.... You climb the ladder...and out the tree.... You wave farewell to the crone and return to the circle....

When you are ready, slowly open your eyes and join us again in the circle.

Participants, Places and Ritual Objects

In the Community, the old crones are charged with carrying out the crone ritual. Any woman fifty-six year old or older and post-menopausal is eligible to be a crone. You may want to set your own criteria.

Participants

All the other women are encouraged to participate in honoring the new crones. In addition, female members of the new crones' family and friends are often invited to attend. It's particularly appropriate for daughters to participate in the croning of their mothers; in this way the ritual can be handed down to the next generation like a family treasure.

Places

The room where the ritual is held must be large enough to hold the group comfortably and to allow for movement. Depending on which activities are chosen for inclusion, there should be room for forming a birth canal, doing the spiral dance, dividing into small groups, lying down for a meditation. There should be room enough to sit around an altar cloth. Since even a small group can generate heat with these activities, the room should be well ventilated.

Ritual Objects

We use the following items:

Crone Altar

In creating an altar, we return to the ways of cultures in which altars were located in the home. This room, where we hold the crone ritual, is our home, our sacred space. An altar is made on the floor in the center of the room, and most or all of the evening's activities take place around it.

We reserve a special round cloth of lavender satin, about four feet in diameter, for the crone ritual. You can make a cloth by starting with a 60" yardage (usually available in satin and felt) or by sewing fabric pieces together. Trim or surface design can be added by sewing, gluing and/or painting words, symbols and/or other images. On the cloth, we put our regular candles and any of the following:

THE RITUAL

* a special crone candle; ours is lavender with a wreath of dried flowers around its base

* a vase of fresh flowers or plants

* fresh or dried herbs, long associated with the healing work of crones

* amethyst or other crystals for the new crones

* other gifts for the new crones

* items of special importance to the new crones.

Each new crone is presented with a stole to be worn over the shoulders or around the head. It is made from four different-colored 5/8" ribbons round-braided into a tube about 48" long. Some members believe that the tradition was adapted from a ritual described in Anne Cameron's book *DAUGHTERS OF COPPER WOMAN*. Others say that the ribbons represent the four quadrants of our lives—physical, intellectual, emotional and spiritual. Ribbon colors are a combination of earth, water and sky tones, or they may be four different shades of the same color. Woven into the center is a thin black 1/8" ribbon called the "chord of remembering," which honors all the women who have gone before. The stole is the visible symbol of cronehood and is to be worn at all future crone ceremonies. You may, of course, want to design a stole or vestment that has particular meaning for you.

Crone Stole

One for each new crone. When it is possible to get them, amethysts are preferred. Many-faceted and clear, they are natural products of the earth which

Crystals

the passage of time has made into objects of great beauty, value and power. These are the attributes of the crone which are crystallized in this magic stone of health, wisdom and healing.

CRONES PAST AND PRESENT

Our crone ritual is embedded in a past, in stories. It was not created *ex nihilo*. The stories are many and complex. For us, they begin in the mythic fabric of ancient cultures of Europe, the near east and the lands around the Mediterranean Sea. They continue up through historical Europe and then to this continent. They encounter other stories already deeply rooted here and also brought here from Africa and other parts of the globe. New stories emerge, tragic, heroic, painful, beautiful.

Many of the threads of our stories have been denied us or have been lost. So we are still learning to find and tell them, digging out research, drawing inferences, sharing our stories, listening to those of others near and far and enacting the ritual. For the past several years, we have been weaving all these together, and the outline of the emerging stories goes like this:

Our forecrones once lived powerful, competent and creative lives, contributing to the material and spiritual life of their communities. With the rise of hierarchies of gender, class and race, our forecrones were systematically and repeatedly denied social power, devalued and violated in many different ways and to different degrees. Many were destroyed. In the effort to survive, many women accepted the roles and values put upon them, even at the cost of doing violence to themselves and others.

Nevertheless, many also refused simply to be victims and both survived and resisted. Patterns of survival and resistance varied immensely among different groups of women and even individuals. Some resisted in the family, others in the workplace or in the political sphere.

Those stories, in all their pain and power, we retell through the crone ritual. And in retelling, we continue to be in the company of those who were victims but also those who refused to be victims only and, instead, chose to survive and resist.

Herstory

Once upon a time...so the stories begin...deep into a past we recreate in our imaginings, in the longings of our hearts and in conversation with those reinterpreting archaeological finds.... Once upon a time, and we thrill once again to stories of freedom, meaning and the possibilities of more just and peaceful ways of living...

Once upon a time, women had power, value and authority. Depending on the era, women prepared meat and skins, sowed and harvested, invented tools for their work, gathered, wove, healed, bore children, defended against enemies, performed rituals and made decisions. Women and men both contributed to the survival and reproduction of the whole community—and contributed in similar ways with similar returns.

Women exercised political, cultural, economic and/or religious power and leadership. They participated in councils or whatever governing structure existed; they made decisions along with men that shaped the welfare and future of the community.

In such societies, old women also held power and status. Freed from the intimate details of child care and the rigors of economic work, they were the healers, the mediators, the wise of the communities. One contemporary crone, Barbara Walker, suggests that a crone was "healer, judge, wise woman, arbiter of ethical and moral law, owner of the sacred lore, mediator between the realms of flesh and spirit, and...funerary priestess and Death Mother."[5]

In those days, sacredness bore the form of an old woman—part of a three-fold visage of maiden, mother and crone. Women reflected and mediated the power and image of holiness. As crone, it was women's wisdom that had holy power. And, some feminists suggest, the crone was the most powerful of the three.

Further, in those ancient societies, as in many Native American societies still, material reality was the bearer of the sacred. Body and spirit were not alien from each other and the body devalued. Religion was earth-centered and bodyaffirming, and all human beings in the clan or community were valued. Within them, for nearly thirty thousand years, crones knew what it meant to beloved, needed, revered and powerful in their own communities.

History/Herstory

But gradually, so the stories continue, transitions occurred, and hierarchical systems—patriarchal, racist, classist, ageist—in the west began to be the norm. Probably in some places the transitions were abrupt and brutal, through invasion and conquest. In others, they were.more gradual and may have developed from trading contacts or as a result of internal changes. In every case, however, the transformations were profound, changing social, economic, religious and political relationships, all of which negatively affected the lives of old women.

Hierarchical systems located power and authority at the top and designated certain groups or kinds of people as worthy of that power and authority. They were conquerors, male rulers or certain other groups of elite males. Depending on the location and period, they may have been Greek males, Roman males, male Christian bishops, men with capital, white men, European men, Protestant men.

Women were denied power and authority and their identity and worth were viewed in relation to the males of the family. Women of elite families became important for perpetuating the family line or consolidating or extending family power through arranged marriages. Or they became a burden to the family. Women of non-elite classes became slaves, concubines, trades people, peasants and/or part of a large impoverished underclass.

Whoever controls the myths, controls the culture, and as Christianity became a dominant social force and an extension of the state, it helped to perpetuate a misogyny, sometimes brutal, that saw women as body and as flesh that tempted men to sin. No longer bearers of sacred power, but Eve—source of temptation, even source of sin. Such misogyny both reflected and helped to perpetuate a body/soul dualism that elevated the mind and soul and saw the body as a snare and obstacle. Christians were supposed to deny the flesh (and therefore women), although according to Augustine, men were expected to do so through self-discipline and women only through the constant supervision of others.

Hierarchy and dualism also meant new myths and/or a reworking of old ones. The old myths of female power and images were changed or de-

CRONES PAST AND PRESENT

nounced. With the rise of Christianity, both "pagan" gods and goddesses lost legitimacy. Yahweh was jealous of Astarte and demanded worship only of Him.

In this transformation, crones lost power, authority and standing in the community. They no longer bore wisdom or mediated between the "realms of flesh and spirit." Past marriageable age, they had little social worth, and they largely disappeared from western history, philosophy and theology books.

But, they survived and adapted and resisted in different ways. In elite and nonchristian families, they still often held power and authority within the family and performed family religious rituals. They ran large households and performed medical and funerary services, applied the science of food production and preservation to the wellbeing of the family and passed their knowledge and wisdom down to their daughters and other female family members. They also owned slaves, women and men, and shared the time and energy of their husbands with concubines.

In elite Christian families, they often did much of the above, including keeping alive the old religions. In some instances, they left their households and went to live with hermits in the desert or to travel with missionaries. Denying their bodies, they nevertheless found a new freedom for their minds.

Non-elite women struggled, fought and survived as they could. Without the "protection" of men and past the age for prostitution, they worked in inns and fields and begged in the streets. A few became craft-people or ran inns. Some, particularly in the countryside, also helped to keep the old traditions alive.

Various accommodations were made between the old and the new. There are many reasons for the rise in the popularity of Mary, but one was probably an effort to replace the old goddesses with a Christian one. Unfortunately, the young, obedient, virginal mother was the antithesis of the crone, and once again old women were devalued and denied power and integrity.

Still old women held on. Some continued to preserve the old ways. Some became nuns and even abbesses. Some worked with their hands until they could work no more. Many lived among other women, and within those circles developed their own patterns of respect, power, authority and wisdom. Convents, for instance, were important communities in which women could survive with some freedom. And convents, which also served as inns and hospitals and many other social institutions in the Middle Ages, brought women into contact and communication with the wider world and its politics and culture, which they were able both to learn about and in subtle ways to influence.

But the war against the old did not stop. The anti-Semitic, Inquisition and Witchcraft persecutions brought new tragedy to Christian, Jewish and pagan crones—to those who questioned orthodoxy, to those who belonged to families with money or had themselves inherited money, to those who were or were perceived to be outside the circle of the faithful.

Old women were particularly vulnerable to the charge of witchcraft. In seventeenth century

England, for instance, according to Antonia Fraser, poor, elderly widows were at special risk to be labeled witch. The Poor Law of 1601 had made the parishes responsible for the poor "by means of compulsory rates levied on its members."[6] It was also a period that assumed that appearance and character corresponded, that viewed old age as hideous and therefore old people's character suspect. All of this, combined with the history of misogyny, made old women especially vulnerable to persecution. "If a man is old, ugly and wise, he is a sage. If a woman is old, ugly and wise, she is a saga, that is, a witch."[7]

Estimates of the number of witches killed range from close to a million to nine million. Many old women were tortured, hanged, drowned or burned alive because they were old, poor and female.

Some, however, were persecuted because they were an economic threat. In the colonies, some of the women who were accused of witchcraft had just inherited money or property. In Europe, midwives and healers also were accused. In part, some of the skills involved in practicing those roles were connected with paganism; in part, however, a rising male professional class of doctors was in competition with that ancient lore and its practitioners. Whoever controls the myths, controls the society. Obviously also, whoever controls the pursestrings and the knowledge also controls the society.

With the Burning Times, the metamorphosis of old women was complete in the mythology and institutions of the dominant culture. A woman after menopause no longer had community-valued roles as educator, bearer of sacred power, wise woman, healer, negotiator, mediator between this world

> *My postmenopausal body has fine wrinkles on the face with deepening lines from nose to jaw; a protruding stretch-marked belly, legacy of six pregnancies; knobby arthritic fingers; hair that has lost its youthful abundance and color; relentless sagging of neck, underarms and breasts. It's as if my whole body is being drained and cannot resist the magnetic pull of the earth, slowly pulling me into its darkness.*
> —Alice

and others. Instead, she was viewed and treated as ugly. She was denied education, and the wisdom she did possess was held in a mixture of contempt and competition as superstition or sinful knowledge gained through intercourse with the devil. In a culture officially separated from and suspicious of the body, she became the scapegoat for its fears and temptations—as part of a hideous, evil underworld at opposite poles from heaven and god and all things good and sacred.

And still old women held on. They brought their weaving, cooking, agricultural skills to this continent from England and Europe. They brought their knowledge about when to plant and how to heal; they brought their experience and their concerns for their children, their efforts to see that their daughters would not fall into further victimization in a world in which they had almost no social power. They brought their fears and prejudices and their own patterns of internalized oppression. Many, perhaps most, identified with the most powerful males in their families or communities rather than with other women. Many saw Native women as savages, African women as beasts of burden, white working class or poor women as of limited capabilities and objects of charity.

And they continued to find ways to survive generally within the hierarchy. According to the letters and diaries of middle and upper-class women, they devoted themselves almost exclusively to the family—managing the household, caring for children, caring for the sick. They turned to sisters, aunts and female friends for help and support and to God for spiritual sustenance.[8]

"Within their sphere, aging women could continue many of the familiar tasks of a lifetime, comfortable in the knowledge that their skills and values might be of service to yet another generation."[9]

In fact, it is possible that this arrangement made aging relatively easy for these women since there were few adjustments to make in their daily routine.[10]

For working class women, the situation was far different as it had been for centuries. Old women had to continue to do business activities in addition to household ones. They "operated fisheries, managed dairies, served as midwives and ministers, and ran boardinghouses."[11] They also worked in the mills, in homes as servants, in taverns and begged on the streets.

For old slave women, the situation was still different. Their story was one of being breeder, worker and sexual object. Those who lived to old age also continued to work until it was impossible. They were denied the one reality that gave meaning, value and some power to nineteenth century women—location in a legal family. Instead, their children, husbands and other kin were sold away. They were forbidden to marry. They and their loved ones were beaten, tortured and killed. They remained subject to the whim of the master and mistress of the plantation.

They also survived and resisted. They had a lifetime of pain and knowledge about how white people did things, ways to avoid at least some of the violence, ways to exploit whites for their own survival. They knew how to sabotage the workings of the plantation, how to acquire a bandage or an extra amount of food. They were instrumental in keeping a faith alive in a God that led the Hebrew slaves out of Egypt. They comforted those in trauma, who were most of the slaves most of the time. They hid those fleeing, and they gathered others around them and fled.

If the stereotype of the old white woman is the witch, or more recently the cute little lady in tennis shoes, the stereotype of the old female slave is Aunt Jemima, the friendly, nurturing, comfortable black woman whose care and concern are whites. Yes, massa! Like other images, it is one perpetuated by the dominant society and put on those who had no choice. Like other images, it has nothing to do with the truth except insofar as it was a role that women sometimes had to play for their own survival and the survival of their families.

The stories of old Native women on this continent embody still other themes. At the time of the first encounters with whites, old Indigenous women were respected, honored, powerful members of their clans and nations. In many nations, they were invested with the economic power of the community, and they shared with men political, spiritual, educational and healing knowledge, power and authority. They were autonomous beings, deeply embedded in community. Their myths, as well as institutions, honored and empowered them. They were fully functioning and competent members, contributing to the common good.

They gave the white newcomers gifts and taught them how to survive and even prosper in a foreign land—which plants and herbs to use for what purpose, when to plant and harvest, how to skin animals and use all their parts. They sheltered white women and men and allowed, even invited them to live among them. They also sheltered the fleeing slaves, fed and healed them and invited them to live with them.

With forced conversions, genocide and then reservations, many old Native women and men tried to keep the old ways alive, passing them down from one generation to the next. They became part of an underground network of wisdom, similar to their counterparts in early Europe. Some became Christian but resisted the Christian insistence on one truth and found ways to accommodate the old and the new. They fought the whites and marched the long marches of cold and hunger and a melancholy of spirit that was almost too much to bear. And they lay down along the way and died, too tired, too starved to continue.

By and large, the relationships among the three groups of old women were shaped by the prevailing patterns of the times. In light of a growing racism, many, perhaps most—white women saw themselves superior to slave and Indigenous women and lived out the stereotypes and violence familiar to them. Even many of the white women who became active in the Abolitionist movement and then the nineteenth century feminist movement were unable to be free of racism and the manipulations of men in positions of significant social power. Survival and resistance too often meant playing by the rules of the dominant class, and those rules always included permission to divide and conquer.

And yet, perhaps there were some alliances made, some bridges over almost unbridgeable gulfs. We don't yet have very many of those stories; perhaps we never will. Or perhaps they must wait until those of us now the bearers of this past can begin to make some alliances. Then new memories of other stories may emerge. The imperative to survive and resist continues today.

Further, much, too much, is still missing from these stories: The stories of other old women—Asian-American women, refugee women, the more specific stories of the many groups of European and Russian immigrant women. We don't have many stories of old disabled women, and although we have stories of women in community, we don't have many stories of old lesbian women. We don't know these stories. We have yet to find them in ourselves or women have not come to Community from those traditions and shared them. As we gather them, they too will become part of the ritual.

Our Lives Today

The lives of old women today are shaped by the two-fold reality of our forecrones—structures of oppression, including ageism and multiple ways of surviving and resisting.

Interlocked Structures of Oppression

Ageism—structures of power and patterns of beliefs and values that cripple and make invisible old people. In this society, ageism is joined with sexism, racism, classism, heterosexism, ableism and other structures so that it shapes the lives of different groups of people differently.

In Maine, for instance, there is a higher percentage of poor people among those aged sixty and over than in the total population. Within that population, women are more likely to be poor than men. The women are also more likely to be living alone than the men. And they are more likely to rent and not own cars than men. Even among women the situation varies considerably. Old women with higher levels of income are much more likely to still be living with a partner and co-own their homes and cars.[12] So while old people in general are more likely to be poor than others, women are more likely to be poor than men and class differences among women will also have an obvious impact.

Citing this kind of variation in no way denies the material poverty facing many old women. Many simply do not have sufficient income for bare survival. Some of us live without heat, without nutritious food, without lights, without medical attention, in hovels. We are poor and we die before our time.

Other realities twine around old women's lives in similarly complex and even contradictory ways. Many of us have experienced or have observed others being patronized, ignored, silenced, for instance. It seems as if the older we get, the more we are treated either as if we are children or are not there. Doctors talk about us rather than to us; we are metaphorically patted on the head for some insight or witticism as if we had done something totally out of character. We are called by our first names, sometimes for the first time in our adult lives.

These are humiliating and infuriating experiences. They disempower and/or objectify and stereotype us. Both the reality and its meaning also varies among different groups of women. For some, it is a continuation of a lifetime of being called only by one's first name, while those who live in very wealthy or socially prestigious contexts may not experience it at all—although other ways may be found to trivialize them.

Given this complex intertwining of the patterns within which we live and which shape us, can we make some generalizations about the reality of ageism?

Stereotypes about old women abound, although

they are primarily about white and middle class women and then extended on occasion to other groups of women. Many of the stereotypes make old women childish (and also do a disservice to children) or feeble or even infantile. We can't cope; we need someone to look after us. Sometimes the stereotypes are "prettified"—we are cute, the little old lady in tennis shoes, she is like a little bird, perky or pert. They all have the effect of denying us agency, initiative, power.

We are aunts and grandmothers. Sometimes and in some cultures, those titles are honoring and empowering. They acknowledge status, wisdom and what cronehood is all about. They can also be reductionistic, perpetuating the idea that we are only extensions of the family, who exist to help or serve those at the center.

Ageism has been perpetuated professionally by making the natural process of aging a disease and equating health with young adulthood. As we age, we lose calcium, fertility, strength, estrogen, beauty, eros, hips, knees and the ability to do 500 consecutive push-ups. The aging process is seldom described in terms of changes and continuities rather than losses. It is seldom seen, therefore, as another stage in a life's journey.

There are at least two other generalizations about ageism that many of us experience. One is that corporations spend billions to reinforce the norm of youth and urge us to spend money to try to pretend that we are still young. The second is that there are few positive images, models or roles for us in this society. There is either trivialization or silence.

Now again, the norm is not only youth. It is also

When I was 37, and in the midst of the most difficult decade of my life, I was stronger and more agile physically, but I was also not nearly as friendly with my body, and so, in important ways, I feel much better, even physically, now.
　　　—Louise

affluent and sexist youth. It assumes we have money to spend on being young; it assumes we want to be appealing to men as we were expected to be in our teens and twenties; and it assumes that after we have reached 56 or 65 or some other age, our identities are related primarily to leisure, caring for/enjoying other people's children, being spectators of others' lives and becoming increasingly feeble. It denies that we may have to struggle to survive, can have rich and rewarding sexual and interpersonal lives with men and/or with women, can challenge injustice, can significantly serve a wider community, can deepen and intensify a spiritual grounding to our lives, can be wise and angry leaders, can lead or participate in a revolt.

Certainly a part of this dominant pattern is due to a tremendous silence about death, which is itself rooted in the dualistic and hierarchical structures we have inherited. As a result, there is for many of us a profound alienation from our bodies, the processes of our bodies, the beginnings and endings of our bodily existences. The dominant legacy is that humanity [sic] is above nature and controls it. The reality, of course, is that death is not subject to human control. The alternative is then to deny it, and that conspiracy of silence has to some extent shaped all of us. Even though as white middle class women, we have been defined as body, it has been a stereotypical definition. We have been defined as sex object and caregiver in relation to a dominant class of men; we have also been defined as pure and virtuous and civilized in relation to other women and men. Neither definition helps us affirm and be our bodies.

An overarching result of ageism is marginalization and powerlessness. How can we use the margins to redefine and empower ourselves and others?

In my early 70's I had a bad bout of arthritis in my hip and couldn't walk. I had to use a wheelchair, and I was scared. The doctors said I wouldn't walk again, but here I am -- walking. I cured it through visualization. A great lesson for me in the value of mind/body connection in the healing process.
—Alysan

Survival and Resistance—Working for Justice

Who controls the myth controls the culture. Through our reflection together, our actions outside of Community and through the ritual itself, we are creating new myths—and new politics. Essential to that process is going beneath and beyond the stereotypes and the social construction of aging to create other understandings. In this ongoing exploration, a number of dimensions of aging have emerged.

One is that aging is a multiple reality. There are many old ages, as many or more than the stages of infancy, childhood, young adulthood, mature adulthood. Other things being equal, our lives at sixty are significantly different from what they are at eighty or one hundred. Our capacities are different; we look different; our interests are different. Right now, for many of us, this difference is a mystery. We cannot conceptualize it. It is not automatic, for instance, that we have more physical endurance or strength at age sixty than at eighty. We are still too much shaped by the dominant stereotypes and expectations. Some of us have more physical abilities in our sixties than we did in our forties, and we simply do not know what is possible in the future.

Most of us don't have a clue about what it means to be old, to be a crone. We are inventing ourselves as we go along. This lack of direction and models can be extremely anxiety-producing. Three of us who have been professional women and are now "retired" feel particularly directionless and anxious as we cast around for who and what we are/want to become.

Further, we are such different places in our own lives. Some of us, as was just mentioned, are addressing retirement. Others are emerging from

When I buy something, I worry about whether I'll get my money's worth -- like a pair of skis -- will I really be able to use them?
   —Charlotte

homemaking responsibilities and are just beginning school, career, pursuing a long-deferred interest. One of us went to art school and just now has become a sculptor and a reporter on a local newspaper. She is an economic provider for the first time in her life, while at least two of us who have retired are facing significant loss of income for the first time.

One reality that seems to be emerging is a freedom (for some it is a new freedom) from expectations and a freedom both to become who one really is and to work for that freedom for/with others. There is a real commitment to justice for all, including the natural world. The decision of five of us to found Astarte Shell Press was rooted in such a commitment. Several of us are active in cross-cultural and class alliance work in Maine and eastern Canada. Others are active in various justice organizations and grassroots politics.

The responsibility of caring for others has changed more and more to caring for myself.
—Betty

At the same time, many of us are trying to learn to take more time for ourselves, to reduce the tendency to work or be activist all the time. This may be one of the hardest tasks we face! Some of us live alone; most of us are in partnered relationships, lesbian or heterosexual. All of us have deep friendships—or the potential for them if we are willing to take the time to develop them. A part of the wisdom emerging among us is that the nurture of our own lives can be a priority, if we choose.

We are also scared about the future. We are probably most scared about finances and mental and/or physical disabilities. One of the current weaknesses in the Community membership is a lack of women with disabilities. We need to talk with and learn from women who have addressed those issues and have not only survived but live rich and meaningful lives.

And we all wonder how we will greet death. Alice Walker's description of Mrs. Davis' dying of old age is an inspiration. Walker writes that Mrs. Davis lay in bed, where she could see out the window, constantly visited by friends with whom she shared memories and concerns. "Her white hair gleamed against her kissable black skin, and her bed was covered with one of the most intricately patterned quilts I'd ever seen."[13] Walker than reflects: "I thought of her dying one of the most reassuring events I'd ever witnessed. She was calm, she seemed ready, her affairs were in order. She was respected and loved. In short, Mrs. Davis was having an excellent death."[14]

Walker's description is set in the context of an essay about the prevalence of toxins in the earth and air and food that prevent us from dying of old age. She concludes, "[i]t must become a right of every person to die of old age."[15]

Walker's conviction is echoed in us. Our growing old presents us with new challenges and with new perspectives on old ones. It provides us with new insights into the complexities and interstructuredness of ecological and economic challenges, for instance. It also confronts us with new challenges and ways of meeting them. Perhaps we can create alternative institutions that celebrate and empower ourselves as we continue to grow old. We can buy a building or buildings, design the space in light of ecological concerns and set our own rules. We can make it affordable for anyone, live as we want to live, make it largely sustainable and yet a part of a wider community—a resident owned "old folks home!"

CRONES PAST AND PRESENT

The crones in the Community are learning that old age is a time of ongoing discovery and challenges, of multiple and diverse experiences and developments. It can be a time of great richness and satisfaction. It can also be a time of violence, fear, loneliness and deprivation. Many of us feel that we are pioneers into a still largely unexplored territory. Perhaps at this stage of our journeys, as in the other stages, in the struggle is life. The ritual offers us support, new insight, power and courage for the struggle!

I feel stronger within myself now, more sure that I can survive what life brings to me.
—Nancy

NOTES

1. Z. Budapest, THE HOLY BOOK OF WOMEN'S MYSTERIES (Los Angeles: Susan B. Anthony Coven Number One, 1980), p. 62.
2. The activity we call the "decades" is described in detail in the next chapter.
3. For a further discussion of ageism, please see the last chapter.
4. Starhawk, TRUTH OR DARE: ENCOUNTERS WITH POWER, AUTHORITY, AND MYSTERY (San Francisco: Harper and Row Publishers, 1987), p. 112.
5. Barbara G. Walker, THE CRONE: WOMEN OF AGE, WISDOM, AND POWER (San Francisco: Harper and Row, 1985), p. 32.
6. Antonia Frazer, THE WEAKER VESSEL: WOMAN'S LOT IN SEVENTEENTH CENTURY ENGLAND (New York: Random, 1985), p. 100.
7. Walker, op. cit., p. 122.
8. Terri L. Premo, WINTER FRIENDS: WOMEN GROWING OLDER IN THE NEW REPUBLIC, 1785—1835 (Urbana: University of Illinois Press, 1990), p. 46.
9. Ibid.
10. Ibid., p. 48.
11. Ibid., p. 132.
12. Bureau of Elder and Adult Services, DEMOGRAPHICS OF MAINE'S ELDERLY: INCOME LEVELS, AGE, GENDER, MARITAL STATUS, HOUSEHOLD SIZE, AND LIVING ARRANGEMENTS (Augusta: Maine Department of Human Services, 1991), pp. 17-9.
13. Alice Walker, LIVING BY THE WORD: SELECTED WRITINGS, 1973—1987 (Orlando: Harcourt Brace Jovanovich, 1984), pp. 35-36.
14. Ibid., p. 36.
15. Ibid.

BIBLIOGRAPHY

Achterberg, Jeanne. WOMAN AS HEALER. Boston: Shambhala Publications, Inc. 1991.

Fraser, Antonia. THE WEAKER VESSEL: WOMAN'S LOT IN SEVENTEENTH CENTURY ENGLAND. New York: Random, 1985.

Gadon, Elinor W. THE ONCE AND FUTURE GODDESS: A SYMBOL FOR OUR TIME. New York: Harper and Row, 1989.

Macdonald, Barbara, with Rich, Cynthia. LOOK ME IN THE EYE: OLD WOMEN, AGING AND AGEISM. San Francisco: Spinsters, Ink., 1983.

Premo, Terri L. WINTER FRIENDS: WOMEN GROWING OLDER IN THE NEW REPUBLIC, 1785-1835. Urbana: University Illinois Press, 1990.

Stephenson, June. WOMEN'S ROOTS: STATUS AND ACHIEVEMENTS IN WESTERN CIVILIZATION, 3rd edition. Napa: Diemer-Smith Publishing Co, 1988.

Walker, Barbara G. THE CRONE: WOMEN OF AGE, WISDOM AND POWER. San Francisco: Harper and Row, 1985.

—————, THE WOMAN'S ENCYCLOPEDIA OF MYTHS AND SECRETS. San Francisco: Harper and Row, 1983.

Editor Edna Ward is a crone and member of the Portland Community. Professor Emerita of psychology at Emerson College, Boston, she is planning to move to Maine with her partner and two cats.

Illustrator Sylvia Sims is a crone and member of the Portland Community. A partner of the Astarte Shell Press, she combines the two careers of graphic arts and nursing.